What is Kumon?

Kumon is the world's largest supplemental education provider and a leader in producing outstanding results. After-school programs in math and reading at Kumon Centers around the globe have been helping children succeed for 50 years.

Kumon Workbooks represent just a fraction of our complete curriculum of preschool-to-college-level material assigned at Kumon Centers under the supervision of trained Kumon Instructors.

The Kumon Method enables each child to progress successfully by practicing material until concepts are mastered and advancing in small, manageable increments. Instructors carefully assign materials and pace advancement according to the strengths and needs of each individual student.

Students usually attend a Kumon Center twice a week and practice at home the other five days. Assignments take about twenty minutes.

Kumon helps students of all ages and abilities master the basics, improve concentration and study habits, and build confidence.

How did Kumon begin?

IT ALL BEGAN IN JAPAN 50 YEARS AGO when a parent and teacher named Toru Kumon found a way to help his son Takeshi do better in school. At the prompting of his wife, he created a series of short assignments that his son could complete successfully in less than 20 minutes a day and that would ultimately make high school math easy. Because each was just a bit more challenging than the last, Takeshi was able to master the skills and gain the confidence to keep advancing.

This unique self-learning method was so successful that Toru's son was able to do calculus by the time he was in the sixth grade. Understanding the value of good reading comprehension, Mr. Kumon then developed a reading program employing the same method. His programs are the basis and inspiration of those offered at Kumon Centers today under the expert guidance of professional Kumon Instructors.

Mr. Toru Kumon
Founder of Kumon

What can Kumon do for my child?

Kumon is geared to children of all ages and skill levels. Whether you want to give your child a leg up in his or her schooling, build a strong foundation for future studies or address a possible learning problem, Kumon provides an effective program for developing key learning skills given the strengths and needs of each individual child.

What makes Kumon so different?

Kumon uses neither a classroom model nor a tutoring approach. It's designed to facilitate self-acquisition of the skills and study habits needed to improve academic performance. This empowers children to succeed on their own, giving them a sense of accomplishment that fosters further achievement. Whether for remedial work or enrichment, a child advances according to individual ability and initiative to reach his or her full potential. Kumon is not only effective, but also surprisingly affordable.

What is the role of the Kumon Instructor?

Kumon Instructors regard themselves more as mentors or coaches than teachers in the traditional sense. Their principal role is to provide the direction, support and encouragement that will guide the student to performing at 100% of his or her potential. Along with their rigorous training in the Kumon Method, all Kumon Instructors share a passion for education and an earnest desire to help children succeed.

KUMON FOSTERS:

- A mastery of the basics of reading and math
- Improved concentration and study habits
- Increased self-discipline and self-confidence
- A proficiency in material at every level
- Performance to each student's full potential
- A sense of accomplishment

 GETTING STARTED IS EASY. Just call us at 877.586.6671 or visit kumon.com to request our free brochure and find a Kumon Center near you. We'll direct you to an Instructor who will be happy to speak with you about how Kumon can address your child's particular needs and arrange a free placement test. There are more than 1,700 Kumon Centers in the U.S. and Canada, and students may enroll at any time throughout the year, even summer. Contact us today.

FIND OUT MORE ABOUT KUMON MATH & READING CENTERS.
Receive a free copy of our parent guide, *Every Child an Achiever,* by visiting kumon.com/go.survey or calling **877.586.6671**

What Time Is It?

1 o'clock to 12 o'clock

Name

Date

■ Look at each clock. Then trace the time in each ☐ .

| 1 o'clock |

| 2 o'clock |

| 3 o'clock |

| 4 o'clock |

| 5 o'clock |

| 6 o'clock |

■ Look at each clock. Then trace the time in each ☐.

7 o'clock

8 o'clock

9 o'clock

10 o'clock

11 o'clock

12 o'clock

2 What Time Is It?

1 o'clock to 12 o'clock

Name

Date

■ Look at each clock. Then write the time in each ☐ .

o'clock

o'clock

o'clock

o'clock

o'clock

o'clock

■ Look at each clock. Then write the time in each ⬚ .

o'clock

o'clock

o'clock

o'clock

o'clock

o'clock

What Time Is It?

1:00 to 12:00

Name

Date

■ Look at each clock. Then trace the time in each ⬛.

1:00

2:00

3:00

4:00

5:00

6:00

■ Look at each clock. Then trace the time in each [   ].

7 : 00

8 : 00

9 : 00

10 : 00

11 : 00

12 : 00

What Time Is It?

1:00 to 12:00

Name

Date

■ Look at each clock. Then write the time in each ☐ .

:00

:00

:00

:00

:00

:00

■ Look at each clock. Then write the time in each ⬚ .

:00

:00

:00

:00

:00

:00

5 Writing Numbers
1 to 60

Name

Date

■ Trace the numbers in order.

1	2	3	4	5	6	7	8	9	10
11	12	13	14	15	16	17	18	19	20
21	22	23	24	25	26	27	28	29	30
31	32	33	34	35	36	37	38	39	40
41	42	43	44	45	46	47	48	49	50
51	52	53	54	55	56	57	58	59	60

■ Trace the gray number and fill in the missing numbers.

1	2		4		6	7			10
	12			15	16		18		20
		23		25	26		28	29	
31			34	35		37		39	
41	42			45			48		50
		53	54		56	57		59	

Writing Numbers
1 to 60

Name

Date

■ Trace the gray number and fill in the missing numbers.

1	2	3		5			8	9	
11		13	14			17		19	
21	22		24			27			30
	32	33			36		38		40
		43	44		46	47		49	
51	52			55			58		60

■ Write the numbers from 1 to 60.

1	2	3	4	5	6	7	8	9	10
11	12	13	14	15	16	17	18	19	20
21	22	23	24	25	26	27	28	29	30
31	32	33	34	35	36	37	38	39	40
41	42	43	44	45	46	47	48	49	50
51	52	53	54	55	56	57	58	59	60

What Time Is It?

8:00 to 8:05

Name

Date

■ Look at each clock. Then trace the time in each ☐.

■ Look at each clock. Then trace the time in each ☐ .

8:02

8:03

8:04

8:05

What Time Is It?

8:01 to 8:05

Name

Date

■ Look at each clock. Then write the time in each ☐.

8:01

:

:

:

:

■ Look at each clock. Then write the time in each ☐ .

. . (box with colon)

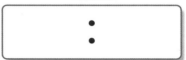
. . (box with colon)

. . (box with colon)

. . (box with colon)

. . (box with colon)

9 What Time Is It?

8:06 to 8:10

Name

Date

■ Look at each clock. Then trace the time in each ☐ .

8 : 06

8 : 07

8 : 08

8 : 09

8 : 10

■Look at each clock. Then write the time in each ☐ .

Review
8:01 to 8:10

Name

Date

■ Look at each clock. Then write the time in each ⬚ .

8 : 05

:

:

:

:

:

■ Look at each clock. Then write the time in each ☐ .

:

:

:

:

:

:

11 What Time Is It?

□:05, □:06

Name

Date

■ Look at each clock. Then trace the time in each ⬚ .

8 : 05

9 : 05

10 : 05

5 : 05

■ Look at each clock. Then write the time in each [   ].

8:06

:

:

:

What Time Is It?

8:11 to 8:15

Name

Date

■ Look at each clock. Then write the time in each ☐ .

8 : 11

■ Look at each clock. Then write the time in each ☐.

13 What Time Is It?

8:16 to 8:20

Name

Date

■ Look at each clock. Then write the time in each ☐ .

8 : 16

:

:

:

:

■ Look at each clock. Then write the time in each ☐ .

Name

Date

■ Look at each clock. Then write the time in each ⬚.

$8:15$

⬚ : ⬚

⬚ : ⬚

⬚ : ⬚

⬚ : ⬚

⬚ : ⬚

■ Look at each clock. Then write the time in each ⬚ .

15 What Time Is It?

□:15, □:20

Name

Date

■ Look at each clock. Then write the time in each □ .

8 : 15

11 : 15

:

:

■ Look at each clock. Then write the time in each ☐.

8 : 20

:

:

:

Race Track

8:01 to 8:20

Name

Date

■ Follow the race track with your pencil. Stop and look at each clock. Then write the time in each ⬚ .

■Follow the race track with your pencil. Stop and look at each clock.
Then write the time in each ☐.

What Time Is It?

8:21 to 8:25

Name

Date

■ Look at each clock. Then write the time in each ☐ .

8:21

:

:

:

:

■ Look at each clock. Then write the time in each ⬜️.

What Time Is It?

8:26 to 8:30

Name

Date

■ Look at each clock. Then write the time in each ☐ .

8 : 26

:

:

:

:

■ Look at each clock. Then write the time in each ⬚ .

Review

8:21 to 8:30

■ Look at each clock. Then write the time in each ⬚ .

8:21

:

:

:

:

:

■ Look at each clock. Then write the time in each .

20 What Time Is It?

2:31 to 2:35

Name

Date

■ Look at each clock. Then write the time in each ☐ .

2:31

:

:

:

:

Look at each clock. Then write the time in each [____].

21 What Time Is It?

2:36 to 2:40

Name

Date

■ Look at each clock. Then write the time in each ☐ .

2:36

:

:

:

:

■ Look at each clock. Then write the time in each ☐ .

Review

2:31 to 2:40

<table>
<tr><td>Name</td></tr>
<tr><td>Date</td></tr>
</table>

■ Look at each clock. Then write the time in each ☐ .

2:34

:

:

:

:

:

■ Look at each clock. Then write the time in each ⬚ .

What Time Is It?

☐:34, ☐:37

Name

Date

■ Look at each clock. Then write the time in each ☐ .

2 : 34

3 : 34

:

:

■ Look at each clock. Then write the time in each ☐ .

2:37

:

:

:

24 Take Time to Enjoy the Garden

2:21 to 2:40

Name

Date

■ Follow the garden path with your pencil. Stop and look at each clock. Then write the time in each ⬚.

■Follow the garden path with your pencil. Stop and look at each clock.
Then write the time in each ☐.

25 What Time Is It?

2:41 to 2:45

Name

Date

■ Look at each clock. Then write the time in each ☐.

2:41

:

:

:

■ Look at each clock. Then write the time in each ⬜ .

What Time Is It?

2:46 to 2:50

Name

Date

■ Look at each clock. Then write the time in each ⬚ .

2:46

:

:

:

:

■ Look at each clock. Then write the time in each ⬚ .

27 Review
2:41 to 2:50

Date

■ Look at each clock. Then write the time in each ☐.

2 : 47

:

:

:

:

:

Review 53

■ Look at each clock. Then write the time in each [   ].

28 What Time Is It?

2:51 to 2:55

Name

Date

■ Look at each clock. Then write the time in each ☐ .

■ Look at each clock. Then write the time in each ☐ .

29 What Time Is It?

2:56 to 3:00

Name

Date

■ Look at each clock. Then write the time in each ⬚ .

■ Look at each clock. Then write the time in each [   ] .

Review

2:51 to 3:00

Name

Date

■ Look at each clock. Then write the time in each ⬚ .

2:56

:

:

:

:

:

■ Look at each clock. Then write the time in each ⬚ .

31 School Day

Name

Date

■ Look at each clock. Then write the time in each ⬚ .

● Breakfast time

⬚ **:**

● Snack time

⬚ **:**

● Lunchtime

⬚ **:**

■ Look at each clock. Then write the time in each ☐ .

● Time to go home

☐ :

● Bath time

☐ :

● Bedtime

☐ :

What Time Is It?

Half past 1 to half past 12

To parents Explain to your child that 30 minutes after 1 is called "half past 1."

Name

Date

■ Look at each clock. Then trace the time in each ☐.

half past 1

half past 2

half past 3

half past 4

half past 5

half past 6

■ Look at each clock. Then trace the time in each ☐ .

half past 7

half past 8

half past 9

half past 10

half past 11

half past 12

What Time Is It?

Half past 1 to half past 12

Name

Date

■ Look at each clock. Then write the time in each ▢ .

half past

half past

half past

half past

half past

half past

■ Look at each clock. Then write the time in each .

half past

half past

half past

half past

half past

half past

What Time Is It?

A quarter past 1 to a quarter past 8

To parents Explain to your child that 15 minutes after 1 is called "a quarter past 1."

Name

Date

■ Look at each clock. Then trace the time in each ☐.

1:15 | **a quarter past** 1

2:15 | **a quarter past** 2

3:15 | **a quarter past** 3

4:15 | **a quarter past** 4

■ Look at each clock. Then trace the time in each ☐ .

5:15 | a quarter past 5

6:15 | a quarter past 6

7:15 | a quarter past 7

8:15 | a quarter past 8

What Time Is It?

A quarter past 9 to a quarter past 12

Date

■ Look at each clock. Then trace the time in each ☐ .

9:15   **a quarter past** 9

10:15   **a quarter past** 10

11:15   **a quarter past** 11

12:15   **a quarter past** 12

A quarter past 1 to a quarter past 12

■ Look at each clock. Then write the time in each ⬚.

a quarter past 3

a quarter past

a quarter past

a quarter past

a quarter past

a quarter past

What Time Is It?

A quarter to 1 to a quarter to 8

To parents Explain to your child that 15 minutes before 2 is called "a quarter to 2."

Name
Date

■ Look at each clock. Then trace the time in each ⬚ .

12:45 a quarter to 1

1:45 a quarter to 2

2:45 a quarter to 3

3:45 a quarter to 4

■ Look at each clock. Then trace the time in each .

| 4:45 | a quarter to 5 |

| 5:45 | a quarter to 6 |

| 6:45 | a quarter to 7 |

| 7:45 | a quarter to 8 |

What Time Is It?

A quarter to 9 to a quarter to 12

Date

■ Look at each clock. Then trace the time in each ☐ .

8:45 | a quarter to *9*

9:45 | a quarter to *10*

10:45 | a quarter to *11*

11:45 | a quarter to *12*

A quarter to 1 to a quarter to 12

■ Look at each clock. Then write the time in each ☐ .

a quarter to | |

a quarter to

a quarter to

a quarter to

a quarter to

a quarter to

38 **Review**

Name

Date

■ Look at each clock. Then write the time in each ⬚ .

a quarter past |

a quarter past

a quarter past

a quarter past

a quarter past

a quarter past

■ Look at each clock. Then write the time in each [ ].

a quarter to 5

a quarter to

a quarter to

a quarter to

a quarter to

a quarter to

Write your name.

by

Write the time in each ☐
and then draw the clock hands on each clock.

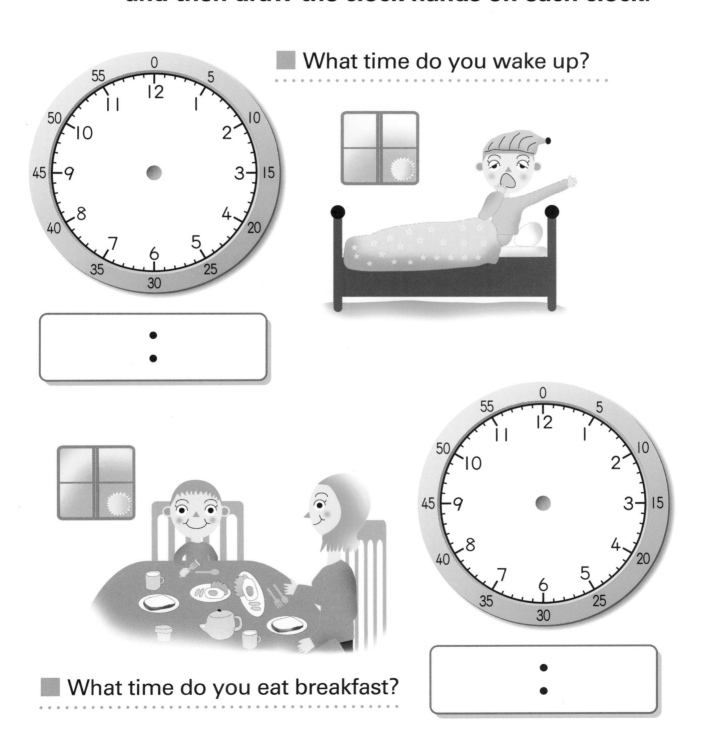

■ What time do you wake up?

■ What time do you eat breakfast?

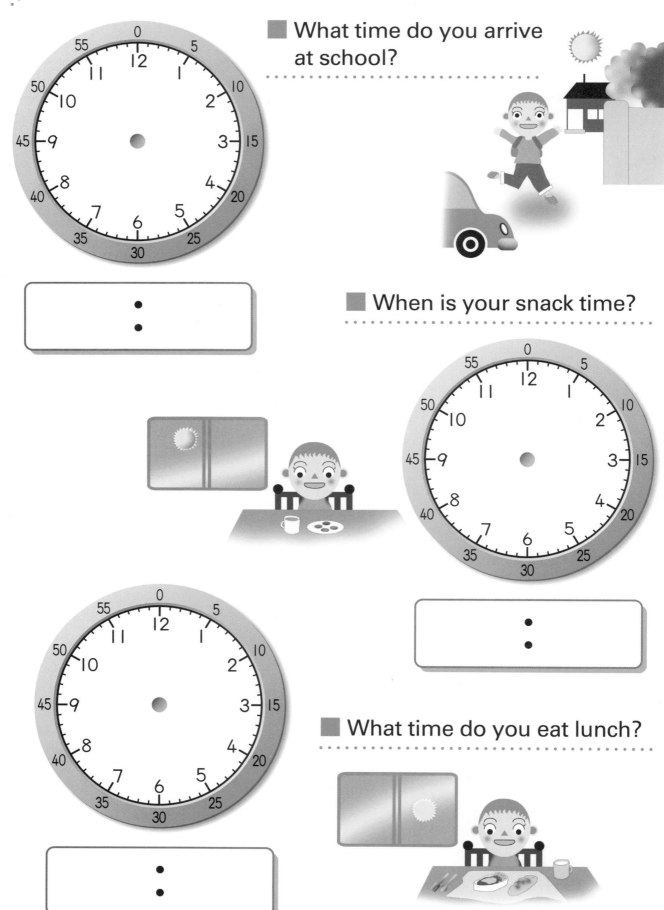

What time do you arrive at school?

When is your snack time?

What time do you eat lunch?

What time do you leave school?

What time do you go shopping with mom?

My Day

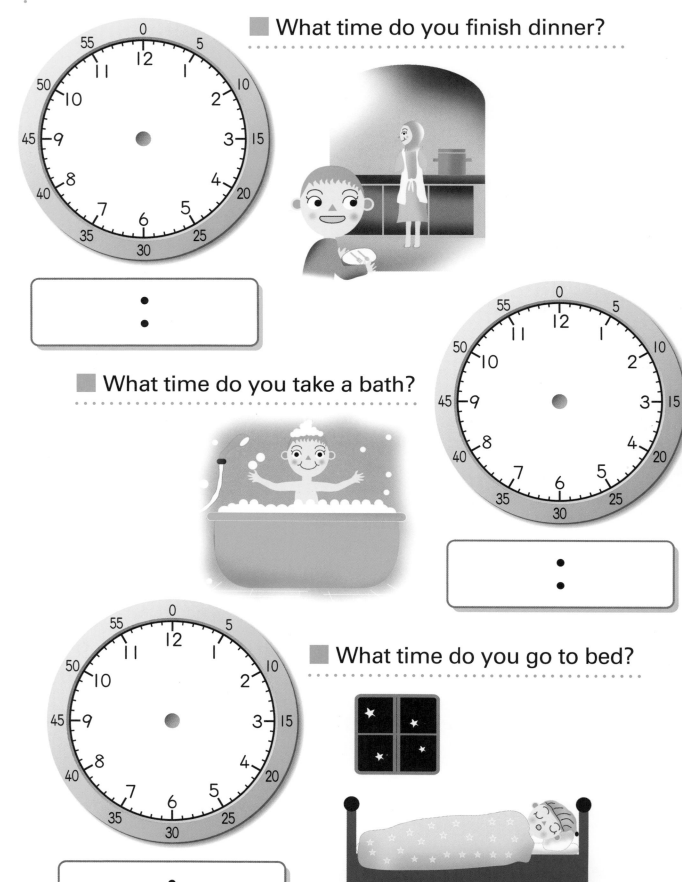

What time do you finish dinner?

What time do you take a bath?

What time do you go to bed?

KUM☺N

Certificate of Achievement

_____

is hereby congratulated on completing

My Book of Telling Time
_____

Presented on _____ , 20___

_____
Parent or Guardian